MW00423572

The
FIRE EATERS

Molding Your Own Destiny

More Easily

By Randolph Michael Howes M.D., Ph.D.

Introduction by Jessie Hill Ford

ACKNOWLEDGEMENTS

Special thanks to two up and coming *FIRE EATERS* Bryan T. McMahon for excellent technical assistance in the production of the end product and to Marge Pettijohn for expeditious and skillful coverwork art.

Trademark for the *FIRE EATERS*, International. Dr. R.M. Howes, New Orleans, Louisiana, USA.

By: Randolph M. Howes, M.D., Ph.D.

DEDICATION

To the "Rubber Tree" ant, to the Little Engine That Could, and to the ultimate *FIRE EATER* who was kind enough to instill in me a tiny spark which I can try to breathe into others.

"So far we may be willing to go: we know what to expect. But no further; for beyond that boundary we are afraid. Our experience makes cowards of us: we want its security even if it limits us. We know that many who strike out beyond this boundary are lost. But not all. Some manage it. And when we envy them, we forget the risk they took. We think that their boundaries have always been so broad and limitless. We forget that they took the effort of pushing them outwards. Effort and risk. Instead, we talk of luck. . . . . . ."

Plato

INTRODUCTION

As you read and reread this book, as you study and absorb an exciting new frame of mind and mood, you will answer two essential questions;

First: "Who am I?"

Secondly: "What do I want?"

Getting what *you* want instead of what others want for you; programming for success; forming habits that will take you where you want to go while discarding habits which have kept you from getting there -- these are but a few of the formidable advantages to be had from this remarkable book.

Dr. Randolph Howes is a prime example of *FIRE EATER* philosophy. The principles he sets forth here have brought him noteworthy success from an early age onward.

The precepts in this book provide clear, invaluable models and examples, all of which can be put to use immediately. *FIRE EATER* philosophy and attitude will bring lasting satisfaction to anyone truly serious about the basic business of getting ahead in a competitive world.

For outlook and attitude has everything to do with

success. It has been observed by the ancients that "He who thinks he can has the job half done." *FIRE EATER* philosophy backs up this maxim with a program of action and with tips for developing the kind of productive aggression that insures results.

Dr. Randolph Howes has spent the better part of an incisely programmed lifetime gathering the wisdom and the message of the *FIRE EATER*.

You are to be congratulated for your own wisdom as demonstrated by your purchase of this book. It will change your life remarkably, so much so that you will know beyond doubt that every tomorrow from now on will be the bright beginning of the rest of your life.

As a *FIRE EATER* you join an elite corps marching along the road to achievement, satisfaction, prosperity, and success.

-- Jessie Hill Ford

COMMENTS

"Dr. Howes is one of the most remarkable people I have ever met. I feel qualified to make a a judgement on remarkable people as it has been a large part of my life in broadcasting to interview many outstanding personalities in all walks of life, from Dr. Werner Von Braun to Martha Mitchell to Jack Benny to Willie Nelson, etc. I drop names so that I m ay make a case for my claim that Dr. Howes is truly an outstanding young man."

Ralph Emery

"An inventor, lecturer, scientist and director of the Institute of Plastic Surgery in New Orleans, La., Dr. Randolph M. Howes is also an excellent country singer and songwriter. With his debut album, Doc Randolph has proven himself a man of enormous versatility. 'Call Me Country' has already been released as a single, and two other songs are possible single cuts. 'Higher Than A Georgia Pine' and 'I'd Give My Right Arm' showcase Randolph's songwriting abilities and extraordinary vocal range.

CASHBOX Newspaper

"Doc Randolph has a history of producing, not just talking - and a bad habit of being successful."

Angus Lind
The New Orleans States-Item

"By day, Dr. Randolph Howes is director of the Institute of Plastic Surgery in New Orleans. He puts on his white smock and surgical gloves and spends the day removing warts, straightening noses and lifting breasts. By night, Dr. Randolph Howes is something else again. He straps on an 18-string, double-necked guitar, drops the M.D. and Ph.D. behind his name and becomes 'Doc Randolph,' country singer."

Joan Duffy
United Press International

"I sorta describe him as a one-of-a-kind. I vote affirmative for any plastic surgeon who has the sense of humor to call his record and music publishing companies *Uplift*."

Red O'Donnell
Nashville Banner

"Dr. Howes' varied talents, enthusiasm, imaginative resourcefulness, dedication to the betterment of his fellow man, coupled with an impeccable integrity makes him a delightful person to know and work with and have as a friend. He is indeed a Man for All Seasons, and we see too few truly Renaissance Men in our time."

Richard H. Steele, Ph.D.
Professor of Biochemistry
Tulane University

"In private life Howes' interests are broad. He's an inventor, a classic car enthusiast and a businessman, who, when not recording, is busy with his collection of radios, and a project to build a model futuristic city from cast-off hospital disposable supplies."

Laura Eipper
The Tennessean

"Destined to do big things...not content to sit in a corner and watch the world go by."

Bonnie Crone
New Orleans Magazine

"Congratulations on reaching such a pinnacle in the music world as well as in plastic surgery. It sounds as though you are really keeping yourself hopping."

Peter Randall M.D.
President
American Society of Plastic Surgeons

"He looked like a man who could mold his own destiny as easily as bobbing a nose."

David McQuay
The Baltimore News American

ABOUT THE AUTHOR

Some people are talkers; some are doers; some are neither, but I am both a talker and a doer. If you are going to spend your hard-earned money for a self improvement book and hope to follow its instructions to achieve your definition of success, then the best starting point is to follow the methods of a proven successful man. I am that man. I present this information to establish my credibility, to demonstrate my talker-doer capabilities, and to let you see the partial achievement record of the original *FIRE EATER*.

Randolph Michael Howes M.D., Ph.D

Randolph Howes M.D., Ph.D.

NAME
Randolph M. Howes B.S.,M.D.,Ph.D

BORN
August 17,1943

DEGREES
M.D.-Tulane University School of Medicine
May 31, 1971
Ph.D.-Tulane Graduate School (Biochemistry)
May 31, 1971
B.S.-Southeastern Lousiana University
(Major-Zoology;Minor-Chemistry)

FELLOWSHIPS
Johns Hopkins University School of Medicine
(July 1,1971 to June 30,1974 General Surgery)
(July 1,1975 to June 30,1976 General Surgery)
Johns Hopkins University School of Medicine
(July 1,1974 to June 30,1975 Plastic Surgery)
(July 1,1976 to June 30,1977 Plastic Surgery)

CERTIFICATION
Fellow: American Board of Cosmetic Plastic Surgery,
1979

PRESENT POSITION:
Director, Institute of Plastic Surgery,
New Orleans, Louisiana
Assistant Professor, Dept. of Biochemistry,
Tulane Medical School
Editorial Board, American Board of Cosmetic
Plastic Surgery

STAFF MEMBERSHIPS:
Pendleton Memorial Methodist Hospital,
                    New Orleans, Louisiana
Tulane Medical Center, New Orleans, Louisiana
East Jefferson General Hospital, Metarie, Louisiana
Chalmette General Hospital, Chalmette, Louisiana
Lallie Kemp Hospital, Independence, Louisiana
Veterans Administration Hospital,
                    New Orleans, Louisiana
Charity Hospital, New Orleans, Louisiana
Children's Hospital, New Orleans, Louisiana

HONORS AND AWARDS

• Selected as a member of the Editorial Board, American Board of Cosmetic Plastic Surgery, 1981.

• Conferred Board certification by The American Board of Cosmetic Plastic Surgery, 1979.

• Recipient: Honorary Ambassador of Goodwill to State of Louisiana, July, 1979.

• Recipient: Physicians' Recognition Award 1977-1980 from American Medical Association for outstanding participation in continuing medical education.

• Selected as one of the 78 people destined "to do big things in 1978" by New Orleans Magazine.

• Invited to present a series of broadcasts on WWL-TV entitled "Latest Wrinkles in Plastic Surgery".

• Selected by the New Orleans Parish Medical Society to serve on 1) Public Relations, 2) Program, and 3) Insurance Committees for 1978-1979.

• Recipient of certificate of Achievement in the 19th Annual AMSA Eaton Medical Art Awards Program Program, 1977.

• Recipient of certificate of merit from the Educational Foundation of the American Society of Plastic and Reconstructive Surgeons, 1976.

• Recipient of research grant from Genetics Laboratories, 1976-1977.

- First in the history of the Johns Hopkins Hospital to complete board requirements in both General and Plastic Surgery in a consecutive six year interval.
- Recipient of plaque and award from Eaton Laboratories, 1976.
- Awarded First Prize-Fifteenth Annual Plastic Surgery Senior Resident's Meeting, 1976.
- Recipient of grant from Eli Lilly and Company, 1975, 1976-1977.
- Recipient of grant from the Educational Foundation of the American Society of Plastic and Reconstructive Surgeons, 1973.
- Recipient of certificate of merit from the Educational Foundation of the American Society of Plastic and Reconstructive Surgeons, 1973.
- Recipient of grant from the Educational Foundation of the American Society of Plastic and Reconstructive Surgeons, 1974.
- Recipient of grant from the Southern Medical Association, 1973.
- First in the history of Tulane University School of Medicine to complete a Ph.D. in Biochemistry concurrent with an M.D. degree.
- Louisiana Pathology Association Award, 1971.
- Top Ten of medical graduating class, 1971.
- President of the Biochemistry Graduate Students, 1970.
- Elected to Sigma Xi Honor Fraternity, 1970.

ADDITIONAL HONORS AND AWARDS
- Patriotism Award, May 23,1980, American Law Enforcement Officers Association.
- Good Samaritan Award, May 23,1980, American Law Enforcement Officers Association.
- Presented the "Key to the city of Ponchatoula, Louisiana", March 20,1980.
- Selected by "PM Magazine" for a personality feature story, June 10,1980.
- Nominated as "The Outstanding Young Man in America" by The Jaycees, 1978.

- Recipient of Certificate of Appreciation from the National Association of Chiefs of Police, 1980.
- Selected by "PM Magazine" for a personality feature story, October 1,1980 Channel 2, Nashville, Tennessee.
- Honorary Captain, New Orleans Police Department, 1982.
- Honorary Deputy, Nashville Sheriff's Department, 1982.
- Louisiana Breeder's Association a member of the American Quarter Horse Association, 1982.
- Presented "Key to the City" Slidell, Louisiana, 1982.
- Presented "Key to the City" Pearl River, Louisiana, 1982.
- Owner, Louisiana Sportsman-AKC champion white Pit Bull Terrier, 1982.

GRADUATE AND POST GRADUATE TRAINING

- Lecturer. The American Board of Cosmetic Surgery. 1982.
- Laser course. Harvard Medical School, 1979.
- Chief Plastic Surgery Resident, The Johns Hopkins Hospital. 1976-1977.
- Fellowship-Plastic Surgery, The Johns Hopkins Hospital. 1974-1975, 1976-1977.
- Hand Surgery course, Harvard Medical School, 1974.
- Chief Surgical Resident. The Johns Hopkins Hospital. 1975-1976.
- Senior Assistant Surgical Resident, The Johns Hopkins Hospital, 1973-1974.
- Junior Assistant Surgical Research, The Johns Hopkins Hospital, 1972-1973.
- Selected for the combined General-Plastic Surgery Residency Training Program, The Johns Hopkins Hospital, 1971-1972.
- Teaching Assistant, Department of Biochemistry,

Tulane University School of Medicine, 1968-1971.
* Research Assistant to the Endocrine and Poly-peptide Laboratory, Veteran's Administration Hospital and Tulane School of Medicine. Assisted in the isolation of the first hypothalmic releasing factor (TRF) under the direction of Dr. Andrew V. Schally, 1977 Nobel laureate.

UNDERGRADUATE HONORS
Southeastern Louisiana University-SLU
* President of the Intrafraternity Council SLU
* President of the Concerned Youth Organization SLU
* President of the Junior Class SLU
* Outstanding Fraternity Member Award SLU
* Placed in Honors Chemistry Section SLU
* Selected as Psychology Laboratory Research Assistant SLU

SOCIETY MEMBERSHIP
* American Board of Cosmetic Surgery
* Candidate for American College of Surgeons
* Candidate for American Society of Plastic and Reconstructive Surgeons
* American Society of Photobiology
* American Medical Association
* Representative, The Johns Hopkins Hospital Housestaff Council, 1974-1975, 1975-1976, 1976-1977.
* Sigma Xi, Honor Fraternity
* American Association for the Advancement of Science
* Society of Nuclear Medicine
* The Johns Hopkins Hospital Medical and Surgical Society
* Orleans Parish Medical Society
* Louisiana Medical Society

FIELDS OF SPECIAL SCIENTIFIC OR CLINICAL INTEREST

- The Possible Role of Electronic Excitation States in Wound Healing
- Burn Wound Sepsis
- Control of Hypercicatrization
- Chemical Carcinogenesis
- Acute Pancreatitis
- Electrical Stimulation of Soft Tissue
- Unconventional Healing
- Spontaneous Subcutaneous Emphysema
- Non-Thrombogenic Surfaces
- Peripheral Vascular Disease
- Electromagnetic Fields
- Energy Sources and Methods of Containment

MILITARY

- Captain, United States Army Reserves, Honorable Discharge, 1976.

INVENTIONS

- Venous Catheter Device: Patent issued on February 7,1978 by the United States Patent Office, Number 4,027,176. (Also patented in five foreign countries)
- Multiple patents pending on approximately 20 other devices, medical and non-medical.

PUBLICATIONS

Howes,R.M. and Nichols,J.R.:An Interspecies Comparison of Intelligence, The Southwestern Psychological Society, 4:4 Dallas, Texas, 1963.

Howes,R.M.: Studies on the mechanism of action of miscrosomal mixed function oxidases, Dissertation, Tulane University, New Orleans, La., 1971.

Howes,R.M. and Steele,R.H.: Microsomal chemi-luminescence induced by NADPH and its relation to lipid peroxidation. Res. Commun. Chem. Pathol.

Pharm., 2:619, 1971.

Howes,R.M. and Steele,R.H.: Microsomal chemiluminescence induced by NADPH and its relation to aryl-hydroxylation. Res. Commun. Chem. Pathol. Pharm., 3:349. 1972

Shoaf,A.F., Howes,R.M., Allen,R.C., and Steele, R.H.: Microsomal chemiluminescence. In: "Chemiluminescence and Bioluminescence", Plenum Pub., New York, (1973) p. 479.

Howes,R.M.: Trouble-free way to insert a Penrose drain. Hospital Physician. October, 1974, p. 74.

Howes,R.M., Zuidema,G.D., and Cameron,J.L.: Evaluation of Prophylactic Antibiotics in Acute Pancreatitis. Prog. of the Eighth Annual Meeting of The Association for Acad. Surg. (ABSTR.) pp. 89-90, November, 1974.

Howes,R.M. and Steele,R.H.: Chemiluminescence of Cigarette Smoke. Physiological Chemistry and Physics, Vol.8, No.5, 1976, pp. 417-428.

Howes,R.M., Steele,R.H., and Hoopes,J.E.: The role of electronic excitation states in collagen biosynthesis. Perspectives in Biology and Medicine Vol.20, No.4, Summer 1977, pp. 539-544.

Howes,R.M., Steele,R.H., and Hoopes,J.E.: Peroxide induced chemiluminescence in an in vitro proline hydroxylation system. Physiological Chemistry and Physics, 8:1, 79-84, 1976.

Howes,R.M., Zuidema,G.D., and Cameron,J.L.: Evaluation of Prophylactic Antibiotics in Acute Pancreatitis. J. Surg, Res., 18';197-200, 1975.

Cameron,J.L., Howes,R.M., and Zuidema,G.D.: Antibiotic Therapy in Acute Pancreatitis. Surg. Clin. N. Amer., 55:1319, 1975.

Howes,R.M.: Making a Portable Drain for Wounds, Hospital Physician. October, 1975, p.47.

Howes,R.M., Lipson,S.D., and Hoopes,J.E.: Electrical Stimulation of Soft Tissue Growth, Southern Medical Journal, 1977, Vol.71, No.4, p.484.

Messenger,K., Howes,R.M., and Hoopes,J.E.: Chronic Orocutaneous Fistula: Report of a Case.

The Journal of Oral Surgery. 1977. Vol.35, P.301-306, April 1977.

Howes,R.M.: From Johns Hopkins: Our Approach to Acute Pancreatitis, Resident and Staff Physician, Vol. 23, 51, 1977.

Howes,R.m., Allen,R.C., Su,C.T., and Hoopes,J.E.: Altered Polymorphonuclear Leukocyte Bioenergetics in the Burn Patient. The Surgical Forum, 27:558-560, 1976.

Howes,R.M.: To Get the Jump on Acute Pancreatitis. Medical Times, 104:53-58,1976.

Howes,R.M., Sloan,T.R., and Trimble,I.R.: An Unusual Bypass Graft for Salvage of an Ischemic Lower Extremity. (Accepted(Southern Medical Journal, 1977.

Howes,R.M., Gaylor,R., and Cameron,J.C.: Radiographic evaluation of acute pancreatitis and pseudocyst of the pancreas. (Submitted) 1977.

Howes,R.M., and Hoopes,J.E.: Current Concepts of Wound Healing, Clinics in Plastic Surgery. Vol 4 No.2, pp. 173-179, April, 1977.

Howes,R.M.: Subungual Melanoma, Surgical Rounds, June, 1978, p.60.

OTHER PUBLICATIONS
- Novels
- Poetry
- Handbook of Medical Eponyms, Signs, Syndromes and Disease
- Catalog of over two hundred and fifty copyrighted songs

PRESS ON

NOTHING IN THE WORLD

CAN TAKE THE PLACE OF PERSISTENCE

TALENT WILL NOT:

NOTHING IS MORE COMMON

THAN UNSUCCESSFUL MEN WITH TALENT

GENIUS WILL NOT;

UNREWARDED GENIUS

IS ALMOST A PROVERB.

EDUCATION ALONE WILL NOT;

THE WORLD IS FULL

OF EDUCATED DERELICTS.

PERSISTENCE AND DETERMINATION

ALONE ARE OMNIPOTENT

Author Unknown

TABLE OF CONTENTS

*"Whimp" is the author's preferred spelling of the common slang term.

CHAPTER ONE

Clearing the Air

You are reading this book to help yourself improve what you are doing and to raise your position in life. If you want to truly know the "secrets" or methods of how to become more successful, then you are certainly reading the right book. Success can be yours if you have got the wherewithall to take it! Right, it is not going to fall out of the sky for you. You have to learn to take it. You have to learn to "make" your own luck. You have to learn to mold your own destiny.

The first and perhaps most important point to keep in mind, is that shaping your destiny is not an easy task. Note the title of my book states clearly that this will make success obtainable more easily. This was specifically stated in that fashion so we can clear the air at the incipience. If you want success, you've got to work for it. You've got to work very hard. Even those who are fortunate enough to inherit great sums of wealth, frequently lose it over short periods of time merely because they are not willing or capable of expenditure of great effort.

By the time you finish this book, I want to have helped to change your whole life, your future, your destiny. It can be done by the simple principles contained herein but only if you truly want success to

1

be yours. You will, however, have to apply these principles every day. Yes, every day.

So, if you are too weak to do so, or if your personality is such that it cannot adhere to a lifelong commitment of effort and energy expenditure, perhaps you should stop here and go on with your life just as it is now.

The old adage that "The meek shall inherit the earth" may be true, but I submit to you that "The aggressive shall inherit its' wealth."

Incidentally, I am writing this book to share with you my own thoughts relative to becoming successful. I have accumulated a record of achievement that I challenge any one of you to attempt to match. If I sound a bit cocky, it's because I am cocky. I'm both cocky and proud. I'm proud to be successful. Many reporters and broadcasters have asked me to write this book. That is why I'm doing it. Also, I have found that within the group of individuals that are success-ful there is a tendency to keep all others down so others represent no threat to the status quo. That is certainly not my case. This book, by the mere fact you are reading my methods, demonstrates that I want to see you reach very high levels of achievement. If I were afraid of your threat, then I would, indeed, keep my methods secret. But, I state again, I want to see you successful also. I want you to know that certain inner peace that you can experience when you have accomplished what others have said was impossible to achieve. I want to share such an experience with you. It can be rewarding in and of itself, irrespective of what the rest of the world may think.

I now want to get a few other introductory things straight. First, I am going to challenge you. I challenge you to change your life. I challenge you to stop thinking about what you want to do and get out there and do it. That's right, either get up off your rear and get with it or shut up. Please don't sit around moaning about how everyone else has so much and have done so much. You can waste precious time with

2

useless bellyaching. Futhermore, no one really wants to hear your complaining if you are unwilling to "get off it and get with it."

Secondly, this book is not intended to be a source book of how to become successful at all things. It is designed to reveal some very simplistic approaches to what appears to be life's most difficult task - molding your own destiny - taking control of your life as opposed to being controlled by the people and things around you.

Thirdly, this book is designed for the eagles, lions and tigers amongst you. That's not to say that you cannot be an eagle in dove's clothing or a lion in pussycat's clothing . What I am saying is that if you are truly a pussycat in pussycat's clothing then you'd better stop right here. The rest of this book will be too much for you. But if you have lion or eagle potential, you won't be able to stop reading this book. In other words, you have basically three approaches to the running of your life:

1) Lead
2) Follow or,
3) Get the Hell out of the way.

ANALYSIS:

BEING SUCCESSFUL   BEING A *FIRE EATER* IS VERY DIFFICULT, BUT YOU CAN DO IT IF YOU WANT TO DO IT BADLY ENOUGH. BE HUNGRY FOR SUCCESS! IF YOU THINK SUCCESS IS COSTLY, THINK ABOUT THE COST OF FAILURE.

3

CHAPTER TWO

To Be Or Not To Be:

That Is The Question

The most frequent difficulty encountered by most people is in the making of the decision "What do I really want to do with my life." I am amazed at the frequency of this puzzling dilemma. I feel that all of us have our own private inner desires, which perhaps some would call fantasies, about what we would really like to do and what we would really like to be. My point is that we should direct our efforts toward the fulfillment of these "dreams come true." After all, why not? It is your life, your happiness, your fulfillment, your destiny. Or perhaps you should live your life according to the standards or goals that others have imposed upon you If you are that weak, then that is exactly what you will do. Remember, many people will tell you that you can never reach your goals or fulfill your dreams merely because they do not want to see you successfully do so. They want you to be as miserable as they are. "Misery loves company." They are actually jealous, envious, or threatened if they see you begin to accomplish great things. They will readily demonstrate this with such trite remarks as, "You can't have your cake and eat it too." Such statements are sheer folly. I can have my cake, eat it too and simultaneously be baking as many more as I may desire. So, please do not let the statements of society, relatives or so-called friends stifle your innate abilities.

If you are one of the many people with these latent goals, than let yourself begin to act from this moment forward toward these goals. Do not dilly-dally around with your life trying to make up your mind. I've seen it happen far too many times, that an individual sits around waiting for his path in life to be spelled out in a cloud message in the sky. They wait around for years to get the so-called divine spark to show them the way. Others take long tours of duty in the armed services or such to "get their heads straight." I feel that 99 percent of this type of activity is totally useless. All they have done is waste a few more precious years of their lives. Let me again emphasize, that to achieve your goals may require a lifelong commitment so please don't wander around like lost Moses for years hoping that a quirk of nature will set you on the right course at exactly the right time and place.

Stop piddling around. Make up your mind - Do you want success or not - To be or not to be. That is the question. If the answer to this question is that you would prefer to be one of the "haves" as opposed to one of the "have nots," then make that decision. Make that commitment. Tune out those around you who will attempt to thwart your efforts or who would attempt to make your goals appear unreachable or even foolish. You can do it, but you've got to want to do it. You have got to feel it inside. You have got to know that deep down inside you have found a certain inner peace merely because you are on the way to reaching your

6

dreams come true.

Please keep in mind, the fact that society even tries to put certain restraints on your goals or ambitions. I vividly recall the story told me as a child that you can be either a big frog in a little pond or a little frog in a big pond." It took me sometime to break away from this traditonal approach and to realize that I could also be "a big frog in a big pond." This may seem very basic because it is very basic. You have got to learn to think for yourself. You have to let yourself be guided by those inner desires for accomplishment and achievement and go right ahead and be an accomplisher or an achiever. The most important point here is to make that decision - to attack or be a wanderer. Only you can make that decision. Only you know your true inner feelings. If you want to reach for the stars, then go right ahead and don't let anyone, including me, try to stop you. It is your life. What do you really want to do with it? If you want to be a wanderer, I'll see you later - good-bye. If you want to set the world on fire with your own magic, if you want to fulfill those dreams, if you want to reach those unreachable stars - I'm with you all the way - Turn to the next chapter because you are a *FIRE EATER*.

ANALYSIS:

IF YOU WANT SUCCESS - TO BE A *FIRE EATER* -

MAKE UP YOUR MIND CONCLUSIVELY AND

STOP WASTING YOUR LIFE DAYDREAMING·

GET READY TO GO "TAKE" SUCCESS! IT'S NOT

WHAT YOU EARN BUT IT'S HOW BADLY YOU

YEARN FOR SUCCESS.

CHAPTER THREE

FIRE EATERS

---

vs.

Whimps

At this point we have determined that you are, indeed, a *FIRE EATER*. You're aggressive, you're a person that will literally attack your problems and their solutions to achieve the molding of your own destiny. Once you admit to yourself that you are a *FIRE EATER*, the whole task of the molding of your life will be easier. Additionally, those around you will sense your confidence, your abilities, your capabilities. When you let them know that you are truly a *FIRE EATER* they will either work with you because they realize that you will become successful, or they will get the hell out of the way.

On the other hand, who amongst you is going to

work with or for a whimp? Who is going to get out of a whimp's way? No one is going to because they don't need or have to do so. Also, can you really imagine a situation in which a whimp has control over his destiny? No way! A whimp is like a leaf carried by the wind, whereas, a *FIRE EATER* is like the wind itself or even like an exaggerated wind at hurricane velocity. A *FIRE EATER* is powerful and makes things happen.

We have said that you feel as though you are a *FIRE EATER*. Well, I want to see you prove it. That's right! I will not accept the mere fact that you title yourself a *FIRE EATER*. I want to see you make something happen. I want to see you breathing fire. I want to see you shaping your destiny. I want to see you working toward your goals every hour of every day. Now that is my challenge to you if you claim to be a *FIRE EATER*.

Being a *FIRE EATER* is not easy, whereas, anyone can be a whimp. *FIRE EATERS* encounter battles with other *FIRE EATERS* of either greater or lesser magnitude than themselves. If the encounter is with a lesser individual he is readily reduced to the lowly level of the whimp. However, if the encounter is with an individual with greater *FIRE EATER* display, then you must draw your wagons into a tighter circle and prepare for battle. That's right. Prepare for war. Reach within yourself for all of your latent fire eating and fire breathing potential or you yourself may be reduced to a whimpish status. These are the times when your true character is tested to its maximum. It is like the final meet of a national auto racing championship. All the slow and inferior cars have been eliminated and there is an encounter among the surviving best. Out of that group there can only be one winner and he represents the pinnacle of success, the champion. He has been pushed by the others to achieve speeds that even he did not know he was capable of achieving. The same is true of your encounters with other *FIRE EATERS* especially if they appear to be initially more formidable opponents. Let these formidable opponents help you reach new levels. They are doing you a favor. They are helping to season you at the art of *FIRE EATING.* You will learn with each encounter how to become even stronger and your newly found strength will, in a snow-balling fashion, add to your overall powers and strength. Thus, do not be afraid of encounters. Remember, whimps have no encounters but you do by the mere fact that you are a *FIRE EATER.* Let your encounters build you. Let them educate you as to what you are really capable of achieving.

At this point. I should offer this word of caution - If your *FIRE EATER* opponent appears overwhelmingly powerful, take time to research the situation, if at all possible. Ask yourself these questions. What makes him appear to be overwhelming? What are his sources of strength and of weakness? Where can you supplement your strength to overpower his strength or to capitalize on his weakness. Again, like battle, try to accurately assess your opponent. Be prepared for all of his alternate routes of attack. Be prepared with your own alternate means of attack but most of all, reach to your inner self for that additional thrust, for that additional energy that will allow you to build the momentum to overrun your opponent like he was hit by an eighteen wheeler. If you are truly a *FIRE EATER*, the reserve power will be there when you need it most. You will not stop until you find that boost of energy that will make yourself victorious. Yes, you will not rest until you are sitting in the winner's circle because you breathe and eat fire. Now, you are overwhelmingly powerful.

Next, I need to instruct you in the laws that govern your power. See you in the next chapter on Newtonian Physics Applied to You.

ANALYSIS:

AS A *FIRE EATER* YOU WILL HAVE NO DIFFICUL-
TY IN DEALING WITH WHIMPS BUT KEEP IN
MIND THAT YOU ARE NOT THE ONLY *FIRE
EATER* IN THE VALLEY AND BE PREPARED FOR
OUT-AND-OUT WAR AT A SECOND'S NOTICE, IF
AND WHEN NECESSARY, TO DEFEND YOUR
FIRE EATER STATUS!

CHAPTER FOUR

Newtonian Physics
Applied To You

Just as all other known masses or bodies in the
universe are responsive to and causative of interactions with all other masses in the universe, you and
I are also associated with these same basic laws of
Newtonian Physics.

There have been some basic laws derived and
referred to as Newton's laws of motion which utilize
some terms that, although we will not get into
scientifically, very well apply to individuals who are
attempting to better themselves. Let us start out with
a simple term such as inertia. Inertia basically refers
to the amount of energy required to put a body or a
mass into motion, to overcome the situation of
motionlessness. Overcoming inertia is one of the
biggest problems that I have seen in other individuals.
They sit around on their butts so much that they are
unwilling to put out the energy necessary to overcome
inertia. Without overcoming inertia, you will never be

able to build up something that we will discuss momentarily which is called momentum, and without momentum you will not have that which is necessary to carry you through life's pursuits and make you victorious over other *FIRE EATERS*. Being victorious over a whimp is nothing at all but being victorious over a *FIRE EATER* will require your momentum. So, the first point again re-emphasized is that you have to make up that mind of yours as to what you want to do and what you want to be in your life and get out there and get it.

This book is not designed as an encyclopedic discourse on how to become successful. If it were, you would spend all of your life reading and studying this lengthy discourse and never dᵒ anything. This book is short, terse and concise for a reason. It gives you the basic ingredients and the basic information you need to get up off it and get out there and get with it.

Go make something happen. Go take something. Go challenge something. Go move something. Go do something. This singular point cannot be emphasized too much because of the mere fact that until you get into this mental state, into this phase of things, you will be unable to overcome the inertia of motionlessness. You will be unable to overcome the status of a whimp. You must take on all of those characteristics of a *FIRE EATER* and make your attack. Not later! Not tomorrow. Not next week. Not next month. Not next year - Do it right now. Today! As soon as you finish this book. I do want you to finish it though, because there are important things you should realize about how to control your newly acquired, let us say, image of self. The new things that you have learned about yourself; the new mechanisms of attack. Plus you have already paid for this book so get all possible gain and benefit from it.

Now once you have overcome inertia, once you have made a lifelong commitment to effort and energy expenditure , to gain, if you will, your dreams come true, reaching your unreachable stars, then we can start to build momentum. We are going to build a momentum which nothing or no one will be able to stop. Because you will not let anything or anyone stop it.

Just as in Newtonian Physics, once a body or a mass is set into motion, depending upon the speed and the mass of that body, it acquires a characteristic of momentum. An example is that at rest a locomotive will do little damage to a wall placed in front of it. It will do no damage at all because it will not encounter the wall unless one or the other is set into motion. However, if we get the locomotive going 50 miles per hour and it strikes the wall, it will go through it with considerable ease, because now it has gained a new characteristic, a new property, because of its mass and its motion. That new property is momentum. This is what you will be building with time, and time is necessary to build it. It takes considerable time. Again, that lifelong commitment to energy expenditure is necessary before you can hope to gain momentum. You must be dedicated, and I repeat DEDICATED, to these goals or you will not achieve them. You will do as many others who think they are *FIRE EATERS* do. They set upon the course of a *FIRE EATER*, being very envious of his course and they find out very quickly that it is not an easy course. We flash back for a moment to the title of this book, "Molding Your Own Destiny More Easily." I do not say "Molding Your Own Destiny Made Easy." It says "more easily," which brings out an important point again as to the reason that it was stated that way. It is difficult to mold your own destiny. I am going to help make it easier for you.

This can be reciprocally beneficial. These other individuals will, indeed, benefit by your momentum but you will also benefit by their association to help you build even greater momentum. Use their opinions, for instance, when they are consistent with

15

yours, to combine the moments of the two, to overcome an adversary or a *FIRE EATER* who appears to be an overwhelming opponent. If you can get enough concensual momenta, then you can well overcome these adversaries.

Another concept which is applicable here, relative to Newtonian Physics, is "that for every action there is a reaction." Keep this point in mind at all times. You, as an aggressive individual, as a successful individual, as a breather and eater of fire, will make particular activities or actions known and others are going to have dramatic reactions to those activities. They are going to act, if they are against you, out of fear and out of a sense of being threatened or they are going to act for you if you have, in fact, gained their confidence.

So, in this chapter we have picked up three important concepts relative to the application of Newtonian Physics to you: Number One: You must overcome inertia. Number Two: You must build momentum and once you have built it, it is extremely powerful and you are to utilize it with intelligence. You are to utilize it to your benefit. You are to utilize it to achieve your ends. Number Three: Remember the law that for every action there is a reaction and you must realize that when you are acting among peers, among associates, among competitors, among friends, this law is always working. You must always be aware of it. This means, therefore, that you must be very cognizant of the manner in which your friends, your associates, your peers view you. Do they view you favorably or unfavorably? Because that is what will determine their reactions to your actions. Also, let both your words and your actions speak loudly.

16

ANALYSIS:

SIR ISAAC NEWTON'S LAWS OF MASS ACTION CAN AND WILL WORK FOR YOU. USE THEM AS A BEDROCK OF YOUR ASSAULT FOR SUCCESS AND IN YOUR DEVELOPMENT INTO A *FIRE EATER*!

CHAPTER FIVE

Nerve, Guts

And Brains:

A Lesson In Anatomy

We will assume that you have now overcome inertia and you have now set out on your lifelong course of building up the momentum necessary to reach your established goals. What else might it require to achieve those goals? It is going to require a few additional ingredients. One of the ingredients is nerve. You must have, even though you claim to be a *FIRE EATER*, the "nerve" to seek out new and daring frontiers. You must have the nerve to explore, to see if your own judgement is accurate. You must also have, if you will, the nerve to assert what your basic feelings are such that you can well compete with or counteract the comments or the actions of your peers. Without the nerve to do these particular things, it will be difficult for you to increase your momentum. It will be difficult for you to continue to build momentum - You will have difficult going beyond what the average man is able to do. You must have the nerve to get out there and take the risk, to take the chances, to get ahead. And it does require a lot of nerve.

The next thing that is required on an anatomical basis is "guts." Now, there is a difference in nerve and guts. I won't go into the medical difference but let me draw for you, if you will, the business corollary of the difference. Nerve is what it takes to get out there but it is the guts that keep you hanging in there until the end of the game. It is the guts that say, "By God, I am going to see this through. I have been nervy enough to start it but now I will follow it through come Hell or high water." This is my conviction. These are my true goals. I have not infringed upon anyone else's rights and I have every right in the world to t. to achieve what I want to achieve. This is where the guts are required. You will find at the beginning that to launch new programs, to launch new initiatives does require the nerve but to see them to their fulfillment is where the guts are required. The guts are what we are referring to in other terms such as "your endurance test." This is where we will see if you are in fact, not only a sprinter, but a marathon runner. And, I want you to be both! Not just a sprinter, not just a marathoner and not just a good sprinter and not just a good marathoner, but the best sprinter and the best marathoner; the best of them all and you can do it. There is no reason you cannot. Not only might you be the best sprinter and the best marathoner, you might be the best pole vaulter, the best high jumper, best shot putter, best everything, if you want to, if these are your desires.

Now this brings us to a third anatomical part that we must consider and that is called "brains." As you get perhaps an indication from this last discussion of guts, without the proper control with brains (utilizing intelligence) one can conceive of a situation in which the challenge is, indeed, exceeded by a grasp of reality.

By that I mean, we are going to have to include in the next chapter a new concept in terms of physics and it is called time. However, while we are considering that, we should think about the brains. If you do not have enough brains to properly guide your building of momentum, if you do not have enough brains and intelligence to select the areas that will be successful, once you have initiated and demonstrated your nerve and once you have made a display of your endurance record with your guts, then you will not be successful. Both of these parameters, nerve and guts, are dependent upon your brains.

It is going to require all three components for success to ultimately be yours. You can well envision a situation in which nervy individuals have no endurance, no guts. They get little distance on the track of life. You are also quite aware of those individuals who have, let us say, the guts without the nerve and without the brains and they also do very poorly in this long process we term life. But, the successful combination of nerve, guts and brains can well turn these three anatomical parts to work in full compliment for you. These three anatomical agents will allow you to overcome inertia and build unlimited momentum. You will be one of the greatest *FIRE EATERS* of them all. However, even with all of these factors working for you, you must be able to compress these into the appropriate time-space relationship. So, please join me in the next chapter entitled "The Time Warp."

ANALYSIS:

ONCE YOU HAVE CLEARLY DECIDED TO PUR-
SUE THE LIFE OF A *FIRE EATER* USE YOUR
"NERVE, GUTS AND BRAINS" TO THEIR FULL-
EST POTENTIAL AND USE THEM IN A CONCERT-
ED MANNER. YOU WILL NEED THEM ALL!

CHAPTER SIX

The Time Warp

An especially important concept to emphasize at this point is that of time. Time, which is a measure of the rate at which events occur, is one of the universal realities of a space-time continuum. Let us now look at the significance of time as it relates to the achievement of your goals.

First, let me relate an anecdotal story to you. My old professor of medicine told us many times that our most valuable possession was time. I can well hear some of my classmates still laughing over such a profound and ridiculous assertion. Admittedly, even I questioned the wisdom of such a statement. Nonetheless, as I have continued to achieve higher and higher levels of success, I can now see and appreciate his wisdom. For instance, take two equally talented individuals: one who requires ten hours of sleep per night and another who only requires four hours of sleep per night. This results in a six hour time differential which is equal to one quarter or 25 percent of the total time in a day. Let us assume that the second individual is actually applying himself all of his waking hours to the pursuit of his goals. It is thus readily apparent that the second individual will achieve in three years what it will take his equally talented competition a four year period to accomplish. Admittedly, some individuals appear to require long periods of sleep in order to function at their best, but keep in mind that sleep patterns appear to be primarily the result of conditioned behavior. Your body only needs four to six hours of restful sleep per night, so do not let it overindulge itself in the motionlessness of inertia. Get it moving. Keep it moving. I firmly believe that this approach can actually lead to a state in which your sleeping brain or your unconscious self can continue to be creative even during the sleep process. This takes years to develop so please get to work on it right away. Here again I must make a note of caution: there does appear to be a quantatative sleep necessity below which your body and mind will both function at suboptimal levels. Thus, if you feel yourself reaching a level of diminishing return, i.e., a lack of sleep makes you function at a non-productive half-awakened state, then you had better get a little more rest. Remember, a true *FIRE EATER* is going to be at his best at all times, so if you encounter him at your half-best level, he will meet little opposition from you and you can join the rank of all the other whimps. Another important point here is the quality of your sleep. If you are finding difficulty with insomnia, it is because your very active *FIRE EATER's* mind is telling you that there are more things you need to do to have made every day truly a day of accomplishment. Please do not deny these feelings. Do not lay there tossing and turning. Get up. Do what you feel you need to do and you will be amazed that by doing these additional things you will have attained a state of transient peace which will allow you very restful sleep.

You must become a veritable expert in time utilization. You must set up your own individual priority sequence and proceed toward its acquisition as rapidly as possible. This brings us to the second most important aspect of time utilization which is the 100 percent efficient use of time while in the awakened state. To illustrate this point, just look around you at the large numbers of individuals involved in such useless activities as small talk with the person at the desk next to them, coffee breaks, luncheons, passerby conversations, discussions of the newspaper headlines or who is going to win the Superbowl or World Series. Unless you are all-knowing and all-powerful, do not catch yourself wasting, that's right, wasting your time with such distractions. Make your time productive. Utilize all of your time working toward the attainment of your dreams. It is only with this very methodical, very determined, very intense approach that you will successfully achieve your goals if you have in fact established goals of excellence, goals for only a very select few. You will have manipulated time such that it will work for you. You will represent a time warp.

An example of the above was my having obtained double doctorate degrees in a five year period, finishing in the top ten of my medical class, investing in real estate, continuing to write music, while at the same time publishing pioneering scientific papers. How was I able to do all of those things simultaneously? Is is really quite simple. It required the priority sequence for my own personal goals, efficiency of time utilization, and near pathological determination. When I was riding the bus to and from medical school, I was reading. My lunch was consumed in a piecemeal fashion between chapters of a book or performance of biochemical experiments. Even my trips to the restroom were utilized as additional time for the programming of my data banks. This type of dedication must be performed in a private manner lest you be locked up in the nearest rubber room.

On that note, join me in the next chapter entitled, "The Power to Self Destruct."

ANALYSIS:

MAKE "TIME" YOUR ALLY. NOT YOUR ENEMY.
IF YOU WOULD RATHER SLEEP THAN WORK,
THEN TIME IS, INDEED, YOUR ENEMY; HOW-
EVER, IN THE REVERSE SITUATION, TIME IS
YOUR GREATEST FRIEND!

CHAPTER SEVEN

The Power

To Self-Destruct

Once you have risen to the level of a *FIRE EATER*, you have developed nigh overwhelming power, nearly overpowering power. What this means is that just as a hydrogen bomb is immensely powerful, it is so powerful that if it explodes, it will certainly destroy itself. *FIRE EATERS* acquire similar properties. Let me explain in the following way.

You will likely find that as you become a constantly growing, pulsating nucleus with the power of a *FIRE EATER*, that many of your initial goals will seem to be only transient goals at best. Once you have been reinforced by the fact that you can reach those unreachable stars, you will rather immediately find yourself organizing a new priority sequence, a new set of goals. You will be reaching a new dimension of thinking within your own mind. In other words, your own mind will now be pushing your very own mind to attempt to reach even higher levels of achievement. As you obtain newly acquired levels of success, you must be constantly aware that you must be able to successfully acclimate yourself to these new success levels. Perhaps an example is now in order such that I may more clearly illustrate the principles of successfully handling success.

Examples are particularly bountiful in the field of entertainment. Instantly, examples come to mind - Marilyn Monroe, Elvis Presley, Judy Garland, and so on. It appears that these fortunate yet extremely unfortunate individuals became the victims of their own success. This is perhaps one of the greatest of all tragedies for it does not have to be and should not be this way. These unfortunates, in my assessment, were *FIRE EATERS* who undoubtedly influenced others *FIRE EATERS* such as producers, directors, writers, members of the opposite sex, and the masses of the people to such extent that the energy of their collective momentum was explosive. Like the H-Bomb it was now so powerful that it was self-destructive. It could destroy itself. Many successful people acquire money or circumstances that allow them never before accessable agents such as alcohol, drugs, mobsters and con men. It, therefore, empirically appears that *FIRE EATERS* as a group are susceptible to a fatal infection with these agents and should learn by the misfortunes of their predecessors.

You must consciously develop your own safeguards to your ever increasing levels of success. Realize that these artifactual agents are, indeed, pathogens that can well lead to your downfall and/or demise. If you are confronted with them, remember that they can, will and do distort reality. They can be directly responsible for the inability to make rational and logical assessments of all factors around you. You risk loss of the "brains" component of the success formula discussed in Chapter Four. You risk the loss of success itself and all that it means to you.

So please remember that many agents, including

other individuals, that you encounter during your success pilgrimage can and frequently do prove to be "hazardous to your good health." Approach them with caution and only rely upon your own personal judgement to regulate your interactions with these self-destructive agents. Do not go through a lifetime of energy expenditure and effort only to become powerful enough to destroy yourself. Stay away from the seeds of suicide.

ANALYSIS:

BE CAUTIOUS NOT TO LET SUCCESS ALTER YOUR PERCEPTION OF REALITY AND THEREBY TURN YOURSELF INTO A TICKING TIME BOMB. ALWAYS BE ABLE TO BACK AWAY FAR ENOUGH TO SEE YOURSELF AS YOU REALLY ARE AND YOU WILL AVOID SELF-DESTRUCTIVE TENDENCIES.

CHAPTER EIGHT

The Bopbag Principle

If there is one singular point that I want to make, then let it be "the bop bag principle." I derive this term from the children's toy which usually consists of a plastic, air-filled image of a clown. The device is weighted at its base, such that when it is punched and knocked down, it immediately rights itself again. In fact, the harder you try to knock it down, the faster it comes right back up again. This singular toy illustrates the type of determination that is required to become successful. Not all things that you attempt will be successfully achieved or accomplished in the first try. Therefore, what should you do? Try again. And again and again. Adopt the philosphy of the bop bag. If you are knocked down three times, then you get up three times. If you are knocked down 100 times, then you get back up 100 times. If you are knocked down 1,000,000 times, then by God, you get up 1,000,001 times until you assert yourself, until you are successful, until you reach your goals, until you touch those stars.

Far too many times, I have seen individuals who had great potential, individuals who had made the decision that they were going to try to obtain success, but they were short on determination. Without adherence to the bop bag principle, without a near pathological determination, you cannot achieve your goals, especially if they are lofty ones. Thus, you must develop the "guts" referred to earlier to bring you through the numerous battles and/or sacrifices you will have to make in order to achieve your personal gratification.

Let us dwell on this point for just a minute. Perhaps I can illustrate my point more clearly with an ancedotal example. I had written, in approximately 1972, a scientific paper that introduced new concepts to the established scientific thinking of the time. In fact, it represented such a quantum leap that I sensed that there would be difficulty in getting the papers accepted merely because of the fact that those individuals who were reviewing the paper did not have enough background knowledge to effectively and accurately assess the paper on its own merits. Nevertheless, I submitted the paper to a scientific journal for review and it was rejected outright. Thus, I resubmitted the paper to another and again it was immediately rejected. I continued to resubmit the paper but also continued to educate my peers as to the contents of the paper. As incredible as it may seem, it took me five years, that's right, one half decade, to get the very same paper accepted. The text of the paper was never changed. The scientific thinking of the reviewers changed such that they could now see the value of this great paper. An important point here is that I had to first have the insight and wisdom to create such a treatise but secondly, I had to adhere to the bop bag principle. I did not care if I had to resubmit that paper 100 times. It was a good paper - correction - it was a great paper, and I knew it. I also knew that it would take the bop bag persistance to have it eventually recognized for its own inherent value. I have now had over 30 countries of the world request reprints of that very paper. I coined a name for a branch of science and biochemistry in that paper and now have been requested to start an international organization based on that paper. I knew all along the paper had that type of potential and I was going to see it through. That is what you have to do, my friend. If you see value to your ideas, to your goals, then see them through. Stick to your guns. I'm not saying "go down with the ship," I'm saying "sail that ship of yours through the storm."

Many, if not most, successful authors can relate to you stories analogous to my story. In fact, many say that you are not really ready to successfully write until you have accumulated a drawer full of rejections. I do not agree with that fully, but I do submit to you that unless you assume that "Bozo the clown bop bag" character, someone is going to knock you down and that is where you will stay for the rest of your life - down.

So, I emphasize again, you may get knocked down in your pursuits, you may be knocked down many times, but you will and you can get back up. That's right. You are such a ferocious *FIRE EATER* that you do not even know when you are whipped, when you are beaten. You keep getting up and coming back. You will win. You will be proud to be called Bozo, if necessary, because perhaps someone or some circumstance can get you down but, by God, nothing, that's right, nothing can keep you down. Stand up again because you are a *FIRE EATER*. You are a winner. You have learned a very important lesson from Bozo the clown. Bozo has made you even stronger. Hats off to Bozo!

ANALYSIS:

"PRESS ON." BE PERSISTANT. YOU ARE GOING TO HAVE ENCOUNTERS AND YOU ARE GOING TO TAKE LUMPS-IT'S ALL A PART OF EARNING YOUR *FIRE EATER* STRIPES. IF YOU ARE KNOCKED DOWN, KEEP GETTING UP THAT "ONE MORE TIME" BECAUSE YOU DO NOT KNOW OR IDENTIFY WITH THE WORDS "TO BE DEFEATED"!

CHAPTER NINE

Brevity And Longevity

Or Intensity And

Propensity

Brevity is one of the real assets of this book. By being short and compact yet directly to the point, it is the type of book that can and will serve as a constant life guide. Keep it close by, close at hand so that you may refer to it whenever you need additional reinspiration, renewed enthusiasm or renewed support for the pursuit of your goals.

I have attempted to put all the ingredients into this book to make you as successful as I have been able to make myself. I have shared with you approaches to life itself. Please accord my views and opinions the respect they deserve. Although an attack on this book would merely launch a counter-attack, please keep in mind the fact that I have seriously attempted to share some of my very personal ideological approaches for the improvement of your lot in life. All I am saying is that if you have the intensity of your convictions and the propensity of your persuasions to become a *FIRE EATER* then be grateful for the help derived from this book. However, if you end up with a whimpish streak, please do not blame me. Do not be bitter. Blame nature, heredity, the universe or something, but again, do not blame me. I did not create you, I am trying to help you help yourself to mold your destiny. If you have what it takes to follow through, then congratulations and welcome to the world of the successful. If you have not got what it takes, then go holler at your mother and father because they are more directly responsible for your basic genetic makeup.

Another final point that I need to mention is again raised as a caution. I caution you to pace yourself; not borrow another's stride. If you let someone else pace you then you are obviously locked to the pace that someone else has established. Do not be afraid to be the pacesetter. Set a brisk and demanding pace that feels natural for you. And above all do not let others influence you to set your pace too slow. Again, set your own pace as it is determined by your inner feelings, by your detailed knowledge of self. Others, meaning peers, friends, or society itself will 99 percent of the time be trying to put restraints on your pace - telling you to "slow down," "take life easier," "don't burn the candle at both ends," "you can only do one thing at a time and hope to do it well" and on and on. This is pure, raw sewage. Statements such as these are made by individuals who still think that the world is flat. Stay away from them and completely ignore their negative influence. Rely on your own intuition as to the setting of your own special pace. Remember, I said a pace which feels natural for you. That is the key. That is the secret. It is a natural pace for you so you can sustain it for as long as you may care to do so. You will achieve longevity because of the naturalistic nature of your personal pace. You will, indeed, have set a lifetime at a brisk, record-breaking pace and you can hold it because it is your pace. You will even find that you will be strengthened by your impressive pace and you will soon realize just how miserable you would have been should you have to perform at a slower pace established by someone other than yourself. Set a pace whereby you are, indeed, running for your life. In fact, you are nearly running scared. You will get far fast, my friend.

Another final point is to avoid all possible negativism. There are indeed, just as in chemistry and physics, positive and negative forces. I feel that we are also responsive to the same positive and negative forces as all other known objects of the universe. Steer clear of the negatives. Be positive, think positive. Represent the concept itself of positivity. Associate with all constructive forces. Avoid all destructive forces.

I push this whole idea of positive and negative even a step farther. I use only the terms winners and non-winners simply because the term loser is so darn repulsive to me that I like to totally avoid it. There is beauty and pleasure in the term WINNER but there is likewise negativity and weakness in the term (I hate to use it again) "loser." Thus, for me there are only two categories - winners and non-winners.

Finally, I am fully aware that I have placed squarely on your shoulders the responsibility of molding your destiny. Remember, I want you to mold and shape your destiny and I want the words of this book to haunt you, to motivate you, to inspire you until you fulfill your destiny. When you do, let me know about it. I love success stories and I want to know that you and I have shared the same inner peace and happiness merely because we know that we are very methodically attaining our dreams come true. I want to know that you have also touched those unreachable stars. And if fate should have our paths cross, I will readily recognize you because now you will be breathing and eating fire. You have become a member of a very select group - The *FIRE EATERS!*

ANALYSIS

STAY AWAY FROM NEGATIVE INFLUENCES AT ALL COSTS, YES, AT ALL COSTS! THEY ARE DEVASTATING AND THEIR EFFECTS CAN CAUSE INCALCULABLE DESTRUCTION. AND REMEMBER, THERE ARE ONLY TWO CATEGORIES OF PEOPLE: WINNERS AND NON-WINNERS!

CHAPTER TEN

Lombarde Revisited

Or Winners

---

and Non-Winners

The late great coach of the Green Bay Packers football team likely has been as effective as anyone in coming up with a quotable quote concerning winning. He said, "Winning is not everything. It's the only thing." This may at first seem truly radical to many of you when you hear or read such a statement for the first time. But, believe me, it is true. If and when you join the ranks of a full-fledged FIRE EATER you will find that you have evolved into a glorious winner and you have also likewise developed into a miserable non-winner (or a "poor loser"). That is right. You hate to lose at anything. You will find that it will even become difficult to participate in routine sports such as tennis or golf with old friends because suddenly you find yourself in direct competition with them. They may only view the game as "a little friendly game of tennis," but you will sense an urgent and forcible need to win. This is actually logical, however.

Let us analyze this a bit farther. You have trained or conditioned yourself to be a winner. You want to be a winner at all times and with all things and you hope to become the greatest winner of all of them. Because of this underlying orientation of your fire eating psyche, you can settle for nothing but victory and the winner's circle. In fact, if someone were to walk up to you and ask you, "What do you do in life?", your best reply would be not that you are a business executive, or lawyer, a doctor, a construction worker, a housewife, etc. Your best reply would simply be, "I am a winner." That is right. That is what I do best - I win. You may well be asked to elaborate on this point a bit further for purposes of clarification, whereby you could explain your answer basing it on your past experiences.

You may have first noticed your insatiable urge to win during a friendly game of cards, chess, checkers, golf, baseball, etc. The game itself really does not matter but the key factor was the recognition of the extreme need to win - to experience that self-satisfying pat on the back that comes with winning. You very quickly then realized that the very same process applied to all of your encounters with life's endeavors inclusive of the spectrum from work to play.

The old adage that "All work and no play makes Jack a dull boy" may be true. My point is that the *FIRE EATERS* of the world can participate in play but there is no goal-oriented purpose. This would indicate that Jack was a real meat head and could have found countless ways to waste his time. If dull Jack wants to waste his life, fine. But the *FIRE EATERS* among you will even utilize your "play" time to sharpen your ability to win.

A word of caution is also necessary here. Let us say that you did involve yourself in a game of tennis with good old lackadaisical Jack and Jack whipped you severely. Please, rationalize the situation first before signing up for tutors, private tennis camps with Arthur Ash, and practice volleying in the hall at the office. Old Jack has nothing else to do but practice and play tennis because this is what keeps this dull character from being a self-recognized dull boy. You should realize that with athletic or physical events or contests, practice is the key. Thus, if you have been spending your time at more goal oriented tasks, then you may have to accept the fact that dull Jack won this one game. But also keep in mind that you are winning at life as a whole and besides you know deep down inside that if you really set your mind that you are winning at life as a whole and besides you know deep down inside that if you really set your mind to it and practiced your butt off that you could easily give old dull Jack a Hell of a beating. But again, remember, is it worth it? Do you want to let this rather insignificant event knock you off the course of your master plan for life. If so, practice, practice, practice, and you will be ready at your next confrontation with dull Jack to play him on his own court and spike the ball right down his dull throat. A *FIRE EATER* could do it no other way because a *FIRE EATER* is a winner.

ANALYSIS

DO NOT JUST THINK YOU ARE A WINNER, BE A

RECOGNIZED, ACKNOWLEDGED, FULL-

FLEDGED, PROUD WINNER!

CHAPTER ELEVEN

Your Friends:

Fate And Feelings

I feel that the most individuals who have pondered and contemplated their destiny have also at times wondered about the role that predestination or determinism may play in achieving their ultimate fate. In having read most of the great books and the great ideas, determinism plays a role of considerable importance to the past great philosophical thinkers. I think that another word for determinism at the present time is fate and I think that fate works, for the *FIRE EATER*.

Let me explain what I mean by this. The *FIRE EATER* does, indeed, construct his destiny. Things do not just happen accidently or by random Brownian motion. He helps construct them. Now let us take fate in its proper context. Let us say, for instance, that even though an individual were a *FIRE EATER*, if he were in the jungles of Africa, it would be much more difficult for him to achieve the things associated with Western civilization than if he were, in fact, in New York City. So, fate in that sense plays a strong role in the ultimate achievement of the destiny of the *FIRE EATER*. I think fate also plays an important role in the contacts with other individuals who complement your fire eating capabilities and capacities. I think that, as I have mentioned previously, when you are in the presence of other *FIRE EATERS*, they either immediately or subconsciously sense your presence. They feel that perhaps it had been fate that got the two of you together, whereas, in fact, it was an intuitive feeling or an inner feeling. Perhaps an example would be more illustrative to the point. I recently had a business meeting with some other individuals regarding what I would consider to be high finances. During the course of that meeting, I had made an acquaintance of a high particular individual whom I had never met previously. Following the meeting, this individual, although we had very little verbal discourse during the encounter, felt a particular need to have a further meeting with me. This meeting was constructed in such a way that it was very much out of character for this individual. In other words, he was not there delivering a business proposal, he was not there delivering or trying or attempting to sell a business document, but merely came because he felt an inner feeling that he should come to talk further so that we could become "better acquainted." This is where we get back to the business of fate and feelings. I think that all *FIRE EATERS* have that basic inner intuitive sense about them that does, indeed, immediately register the presence of another *FIRE EATER*. It does not come up as a red flag in the mind but it is something that is "there." It is something that creates an awareness, it is something that creates an impression in another individual.

On the other hand you may, in fact, be impressed by another *FIRE EATER*. You may have that inner feeling that you do not know what it is about this other individual, but you do know that you need further exposure to him and that you could complement each others' success and make each others' achievement and attainment of success more easily done. Please do not deny these inner feelings. They are far too important. They are, let us say, the unwritten guidelines for the *FIRE EATER*. If you are in a situation with another *FIRE EATER*, that is, one of a contest of wits of the two *FIRE EATERS* and you feel uncomfortable being against your opponent, then I suggest that you either opt for more time or really dig deep down to your *FIRE EATER* capacity and annihilate the individual at that poi

I think that your *FIRE EATER* personality is telling you something. It is speaking that unwritten code. It is saying, "this other individual is dangerous" and I think that you should respond appropriately by either removing yourself from the circumstances of the individual, or by annihilation or by reduction of time spent with him. If that individual you have just met or contacted leaves beneficial or "good" feelings, these are, indeed, the contacts that you should pursue. This is not to say that you pursue this without any caution, but it is to say that you pursue with intelligence. Your amount of time and your amount of exposure to this individual will be keyed to the new factors that you have learned about your new acquaintance or associate.

I just mentioned the word "comfort" related to mental approaches, psychological attitudes, or anything you want to call it, toward another individual. I think that this is where your individual senses that we have not yet gained control of or even really gained more than fragmentary knowledge about, come into play. By that I mean I feel that it is becoming increasingly important to me that my intuitive senses are, indeed, something that I can rely on. If I touch something that is hot, I take my hand away. I am saying too, that the intuitive sense should not be tossed aside merely because it cannot be quantified in terms of Western scientific method. I am saying that it is, in fact, a part of the *FIRE EATERS* psyche. Please do not sell it short. Utilize it. Let it help you. Let it lead you. Let your inner feelings and let your intuition help guide your fate. Let the fate that you create, in fact, help you to mold more easily that destiny that you seek.

ANALYSIS:

BE READY WHEN OPPORTUNITY KNOCKS TO OPEN THE DOOR WIDE. ALSO, LET YOUR INTUITIVE FEELINGS HELP GUIDE YOU. WHEN SOMETHING DOES NOT "FEEL" RIGHT, AVOID IT!

CHAPTER TWELVE

Set A Reasonable

Goal Every Day -

Go Out And

Conquer The World

I think that one of the major problems that we run into in our day to day encounter with life is that we suddenly find ourselves in a situation in which we have extra time; time in which we are sitting around in front of a television set, or sitting around in an apartment or a room and there literally is nothing going on. You are sitting there thinking you wish something would happen, but nothing is happening. This is exactly the situation that you have to try to change, that you have to alter. In other words, you "get up off of it" again and you go make something happen. You do not sit there and wait for something to happen. In addition, not only do you make something happen, you make something of monumental importance happen. That is not to say now, that those things that do have monumental importance do not also have monumental consequences, because usually they do. But, that is to say that unless you get up off of it and start making things happen instead of waiting for things to happen, then things are not going to happen. This is a key observation for any successful *FIRE EATER*. There are few of us or few individuals who are fortunate enough to be able to sit around until the "mountain comes to Mohammed." Usually, Mohammed has to go to the mountain.

At the beginning, at any rate. Once you become an overwhelming and allpowerful *FIRE EATER*, then, in fact, the world will come to you. You can rest assured of that. It is frequently not due to that fact that individuals are made to seek your presence but they will be drawn to the fact that you are, indeed, one of the rising stars on the horizon. This will prove extremely beneficial in the long run. This, however, is also a point at which you will be drawing to you individuals who are out to exploit your fire eating talent, who are out to, if you will, strip you of those things that we refer to a little later in the book called, "the basics of life," which are namely, gold, land, and precious stones.

As you proceed down life's long road to your ultimate destiny which you have shaped for yourself, you will find that the inner peace of your individual successes are indeed rewarding and reinforcing. Also, you will

48

likely find that your fire eating personality will not rest even with your latest success for a long period of time. Your inner self will be either consciously or subconsciously scanning the horizon for new challenges, higher mountains to climb, for farther stars to reach and touch. Please caution yourself at these times and reflect on the self-destruct chapter. Also, however, do not be frightened or afraid to seek newer and greater challenges. My point is this. As you discover your true inner identity, your rapid growth pattern, your cumulative record of successes, you will by your *FIRE EATER* nature be forced to seek higher levels of accomplishment. There is absolutely nothing wrong with this. In fact, it is the ultimate end product of a *FIRE EATER*.

A *FIRE EATER* could never be totally complacent with his present lot, or position in life. He will continue to grow and develop up to the point where his only remaining goal at the beginning of each and every day is to go out and conquer the world. That is right - conquer the whole blankety-blank world! In attempting to conquer it, you will have to discover all the many fascinating and rewarding people and experiences that exist. So do not be bashful, humble or shy. Go out and conquer the world, my fire eating friend and we will meet along the way. I am looking forward to it and I will see you at the only place that we can stop and chat - I will see you at the top of the world. I will see you in your full fire eating glory. It will be a proud, fulfilling and rewarding moment. It will make it all worth the energy expenditure and put meaning to the whole process. *FIRE EATER*, do your thing!

ANALYSIS:

SET A FIRE EATING GOAL THAT WILL MAKE OTHERS SHUDDER AND TREMBLE JUST TO THINK ABOUT IT. YOU CAN ACHIEVE IT BECAUSE YOU ARE A *FIRE EATER*.

CHAPTER THIRTEEN

Get It Or Forget It

There is another catch phrase similar to the title of this chapter and that I would like to share with you. It is simply emphatically: "Get it!, Get it!, Get it!" I would recommend that you scrawl these simple aphorisms on big, bold, red letters on your frontal lobes. Only you will see them, but you will be able to frequently review them, especially at times when some of your fire eating energy has been drained or expended due to either an encounter with a difficult task or a (or any) challenger. You see, I do not want you to just think you are aggressive. I want you to, in fact, be the most aggressive person you know. I want you to represent the concept of aggression itself. I want you to become "aggression," almost to the point that if someone were to ask you your name, you would answer in a stern, confident voice, "I am aggression."

It is this type of aggressive, achiever-oriented thinking that will motivate you to Get it!, Get it!, Get it! (even if you feel physically tired). Since I just mentioned your "physical" condition, let me address that aspect of things for a moment. You do need to keep your body in a state of good health, but let me

51

elaborate on this point. I know people who are so engrossed in being in good health, that they lose sight of all other goals. They transform into another mindless member of the International Society of Health Nuts. Nothing will lead to and keep you in such good physical health more than an overwhelmingly aggressive mental attitude to assert yourself over all obstacles including one called "illness." As we know, 60 percent of today's hospital beds are occupied by people with psychosomatic illnesses. Frankly, either they want to be ill or they are getting some kind of secondary gain out of being ill. Secondary gains can be in the form of sympathy, attention of others who otherwise do not give a hoot, a good reason to be lazy and avoid energy expenditure, and avoidance of all responsibilities. I am not preaching holistic medicine, even though I thoroughly believe in it, but I am simply saying illness is only one of many whimps of life which a *FIRE EATER* can overcome simply because you must. You cannot touch those untouchable stars while laying in a hospital bed. You have got to get out of that bed and reach, yes!, reach out for that star. That star is not going to come to some malingering, whiny whimp laying rather helplessly in a bed of self-pity. I want your whole mind and body so intent on your goals that you do not have the time to get sick, you cannot afford the luxury of illness. Also, I am not saying to drive yourself to an early grave by foolishly overworking but remember this most important basic question, "What, if any, are the real limits of the human body?" That question can be answered in a second. There are no known limits! Each and every year we see a new group of record breakers - a new group of *FIRE EATERS* - destroy the previous world records or limits of our species. Where will it stop I seriously doubt that it will or can be stopped. As long as *FIRE EATERS* exist, new records will be set, then broken, then reset, then rebroken. This cycle can only be a natural followup to the course of any *FIRE EATER*. Once we have scaled the height of the tallest mountain, we are already looking for a higher peak, or a novel way of making it more difficult to scale the just-conquered peak. We constantly seek out greater challenges.

Yes, you did read the chapter title - "Get it! or Forget it!" That's right. If you want to be a *FIRE EATER*, then let us go "get it" or otherwise you forget it and I will go on alone. Remember, I will help coach you but I will not be guilty of spoon-feeding or hand-holding. So let's move it and move it together to the next chapter entitled, "The Latent Power to be a Mountain Mover."

ANALYSIS:

I HAVE ALREADY SAID IT! GET IT! GET IT!

CHAPTER FOURTEEN

The Latent Power

To Be

A Mountain Mover

In all preceding chapters in this book I have purposely stayed away from the more routine approach toward the road to success. By this I mean that I have strayed away from the past programs such as the Dale Carnegie courses or the approaches of EST.

At this point I would like to mention and discuss with you a few of the other approaches, if you will, to achieve success. I will not give you the direct sources for them but, such that I am not guilty of plagiarism, I state categorically, before each that they are not my original statements. Their discussion will, of course, by my original recipe.

The first is the following:

"Many people believe that their dreams can have unique results. Thoreau said that if one moved in the direction of his dreams and really tried to live the life he had imagined, he would meet with unexpected success. A dream can make the impossible if you do work diligently. You must stay awake and make it come true, however."

My only disagreement from the aforementioned statement, which I fully believe in, is when Thoreau says that if you work toward your dream that you would meet with unexpected success. I take issue with that statement. In fact, I take abrupt issue with it because the success you meet is not going to be unexpected at all but is, in fact, anticipated and will be a predictable success.

Let me take a second statement that is frequently quoted relative to positive thinking:

"A right idea consciously and persistently held in mind tends to be realized. Frequently, time is needed to have an idea developed: but it will be realized - of that you can be sure. The power of positive thought is far more than a clever slogan: It is latent power that can make the unusual happen. Clear thinking underlies this power."

I am in complete agreement with this statement. I just wish that I had said it first. The most important statement in this quote is that the presence of clear, positive thought is, indeed, a latent power. This is exactly what I have been emphasizing from the beginning of this book. You do have the inner ability, inner latent power, to be mover of mountains to mold your own destiny, to touch those unreachable stars. I say to you, *FIRE EATER*, use that power!

Use that latent inner ability to move mountains, to

mold your own destiny. You can do it and I know you can do it and I will accept from you no less than to see mountains moving all over the place.

The next passage that I would like to share with you is as follows:

"Things that happen to us are consequences, not coincidences. Once a person believes that he can control circumstances by learning to apply his thinking powers, consciously, he can become master of his fate. No one is justified in feeling that opportunity comes only by chance. 'As a man thinks in his heart, so is he,' is a principle that has been tested many times by men of every nation."

To me this is a very beautiful passage. It again states what I have been harping on over and over from the beginning - You can become the master of your fate. You can "mold your own destiny."

"As a man thinks in his heart, so is he." However, you must believe, wholeheartedly and without even the slightest fragment of a doubt, in your abilities. Always be aware of your true identity in that you are a full-fledged, raving *FIRE EATER*. If you have doubts about it, it will not fly - it will not work. If you have any self doubts, go back and assume the existence and role of a whimp. You must proceed with assertiveness and with confidence, complete confidence in what you are and what you are setting out to accomplish. Visualize yourself and your goal clearly in your mind! Then make it happen!

I will recall a quote of another surgeon as follows: "Doctor, you certainly are lucky to have achieved so much, so fast." The doctor's response was that it appeared to him that the luckier he became, the harder he worked. What he was really saying was that there was a direct mathematical correlation between his energy expenditure and the level of his accomplishments. His success was not a matter of "luck" or coincidence. It was a direct result or consequence of the molding of his own destiny. It was a matter of diligent work, a matter of a lifetime of energy expenditure, a matter of attempting to move in the direction of the man's perceived dreams, a matter of moving those mountains with that latent inner power.

57

Not only did he scale the highest mountains, but he also moved them and moved them repeatedly. He was, indeed, a great *FIRE EATER*. Do you think, for even a minute that individuals from Albert Schwitzer to Albert Einstein, from Alexander the Great to Alexander Graham Bell were not movers of mountains and touchers of stars? Of course not! They were truly frontier makers and most of all, truly *FIRE EATERS*.

Victory will be the reward of the positive thinkers. Victory will be the reward of the positive thinkers. Victory will be the reward of the *FIRE EATERS*. Victory will be the reward of your effort and your energy expenditure because you are a *FIRE EATER*. The spoils of defeat will go to the negatives. The spoils of defeat will go to the whimps. Let them be satisfied with their spoils but let us continue to strive for that special inner feeling, that special reward that comes from being victorious, that comes from a realization of achieving our dreams come true. *FIRE EATER*, do your thing. Do what you do best. Be successful. The terms are interchangeable - *FIRE EATER* equals success and vice versa. Go, *FIRE EATER*, Go!

ANALYSIS:

DREAMS CAN BE CHANGED TO A REALITY AND

ONLY YOU HAVE THE *FIRE EATER* POWER TO

DO IT!

CHAPTER FIFTEEN

The
___

Teeter-Totter
___

Mentality
___

From childhood we are all familiar with the teeter-totter or see-saw board. Basically, if one end is up, then the other end is down and vice versa. Unfortunately, many people are of the "teeter-totter mentality" meaning that they feel that the only way that they can go up in the world is by putting someone else down. They just do not see enough room at the top for others and they will make an all-out effort to keep everyone around them down, so they can singularly occupy their lofty position on the teeter-totter.

Since this is a "How to" book, let me now tell you how to deal with these individuals. First, try to genuinely educate them to the fact that others' success does not necessarily preclude or negate their success. Try to point out to them that there are innumerable examples in which the overall success of a business, company, or group is dependent upon and actually made stronger by the cumulative successes of its members. This is in contrast to strength being related to only one of the members' success. The "teeter-totter mentality" is born out of individuals' own inner or preceived insecurities. Do not let their insecurities or hang-ups hang you up.

If the individual is not open to education then more drastic measures must be taken with diplomacy and with certain caution. Keep your motives to yourself because a dyed-in-the-wool teeter-totter mentality will be threatened by your intent to raise your level and therefore, in turn, lower his (her) level. Thus, move with caution but definitely MOVE. Move up the pole. Move up to greater levels of success and achievement. Let your *FIRE EATER* personality guide you cautiously, but ever so effectively, to saw the see-saw board in half, if necessary. Most of all, do not be afraid to change the status quo - if you are going to advance, it may be imperative to shake the good old status quo. But again, do so in such a manner as not to be too squeaky of a wheel because sometimes squeaky wheels do not get the grease but they get removed and replaced entirely.

Napolean was about twenty-six years of age when he realized that he was destined for greatness. I believe that true *FIRE EATERS* also have an awareness that they are also destined to do great things. At first, however, because of society's teachings and morees, one may try to brush aside or deny these inner feelings. You may wonder if you are not a little pathologically grandiose? Well, stop wondering! If you are a *FIRE EATER* you are grandiose. All *FIRE EATERS* are grandiose, and justifiably so - not pathologically so.

Only through your acceptance of your visions for yourself can you ever hope to realize them. If others brand you with the label of grandiosity, bury them under piles of your achievements and successes produced by your grandiose nature. Turn grandiosity from a misappropriately applied term into a touchable, tangible reality.

Perhaps I should now also point out that there are those loony individuals whose visions of grandiose are, indeed merely visions. They are only the talkers and not the doers. They are whimps trying to wear *FIRE EATERS'* clothing. Their disguise is as poor as their individual track records and everyone ultimately recognizes them as dreamers, drifters and dolittles.

I again emphasize that if the teeter-totter mentality individual even suspects your intent for further achievement, his paranoia will force him to attempt to blow you right off the seat of the old see saw board. This could definitely lead to a *FIRE EATER* VS. *FIRE EATER* confrontation so always be prepared to go to war. Also, remember the prior principles I have discussed related to encounters with other *FIRE EATERS*.

ANALYSIS:

A TRUE *FIRE EATER* IS NOT GREEDY. IN FACT, YOU ENJOY SEEING OTHERS SUCCEED AS LONG AS IT DOES NOT OBSCURE YOUR SUCCESS.

CHAPTER SIXTEEN

See Your Destiny:

Visualization

All of the preceding chapters have been of considerable importance and this chapter is certainly of no less importance. In fact, it may be of even greater importance than some. I want you to develop and perfect the process of the "visualization" of your success. I want you to be able to focus your greatest energies towards your visualized goals. The mere fact that you have the capacity to "see" or "visualize" your means that it indeed, is a part of reality - it has existed in your mind's eye and you can concentrate and focus your *FIRE EATER* energies to turn your dreams into a reality.

Visualization is presently being used in other ways to help individuals in their battles against cancer, breaking bad habits such as smoking, and fighting off diseases. This is well and good and it appears to have at least limited success. However, here I am specifically instructing you to utilize visualization to help you become an even greater *FIRE EATER*, to reach your goals and to touch your desired stars.

Some authors feel that visualization helps to establish a link between your conscious and you subconscious mind. Remember, that I have previously told you that a key to your becoming a true *FIRE EATER* is based on the content of your subconscious mind. In fact, it is difficult to project a lasting charade of a personality. Others, especially other *FIRE EATERS* can readily see through the phoney, thin veneer. I think of the many times I have been asked how did I spend my childhood and adolescense in a constructive manner. The answer is simple. I was basically born an adult, physiologically a child but mentally an adult. Intellectually, I had the capacity to observe, evaluate and accurately interpret the events which were occuring around me. I was able to formulate the frontal-lobe framework to get from point A to point B in one's life with the least difficulty.

ANALYSIS:

VISUALIZE: "SEE" YOUR DESTINY!

CHAPTER SEVENTEEN

Analyses Of A

FIRE EATER

Howes' Hawk Talk

1. ANALYSIS:

BEING SUCCESSFUL - BEING A *FIRE EATER* IS
VERY DIFFICULT, BUT YOU CAN DO IT IF YOU
WANT TO DO IT BADLY ENOUGH. BE HUNGRY
FOR SUCCESS! IF YOU THINK SUCCESS IS
COSTLY, THINK ABOUT THE COST OF FAILURE.

2. ANALYSIS:

IF YOU WANT SUCCESS - TO BE A *FIRE EATER* - MAKE UP YOUR MIND CONCLUSIVELY AND STOP WASTING YOUR LIFE DAYDREAMING. GET READY TO GO "TAKE" SUCCESS! IT IS NOT WHAT YOU EARN BUT IT IS HOW BADLY YOU YEARN FOR SUCCESS.

3. ANALYSIS:

AS A *FIRE EATER* YOU WILL HAVE NO DIFFICULTY IN DEALING WITH (ANNIHILATING) WHIMPS BUT KEEP IN MIND THAT YOU ARE NOT THE ONLY *FIRE EATER* IN THE VALLEY AND BE PREPARED FOR OUT-AND-OUT WAR AT A SECOND'S NOTICE, IF AND WHEN NECESSARY, TO DEFEND YOUR *FIRE EATER* STATUS!

4. ANALYSIS:

SIR ISAAC NEWTON'S LAWS OF MASS ACTION CAN AND WILL WORK FOR YOU. USE THEM AS

BEDROCK OF YOUR ASSAULT FOR SUCCESS
AND IN YOUR DEVELOPMENT INTO A *FIRE
EATER*!

5. ANALYSIS:

ONCE YOU HAVE CLEARLY DECIDED TO PUR-
SUE THE LIFE OF A *FIRE EATER* USE YOUR
"NERVE, GUTS AND BRAINS" TO THEIR FULL-
EST POTENTIAL AND USE THEM IN A CON-
CERTED MANNER. YOU WILL NEED THEM ALL!

6. ANALYSIS:

MAKE "TIME" YOUR ALLY, NOT YOUR ENEMY.
IF YOU WOULD RATHER SLEEP THAN WORK,
THEN TIME IS, INDEED, YOUR ENEMY; HOW-
EVER, IN THE REVERSE SITUATION, TIME IS
YOUR GREATEST FRIEND!

7. ANALYSIS:

BE CAUTIOUS NOT TO LET SUCCESS ALTER

YOUR PERCEPTION OF REALITY AND THEREBY
TURN YOURSELF INTO A TICKING TIME BOMB.
ALWAYS BE ABLE TO BACK AWAY FAR
ENOUGH TO SEE YOURSELF AS YOU REALLY
ARE AND YOU WILL AVOID SELF-DESTRUCTIVE
TENDENCIES.

8. ANALYSIS:

"PRESS ON." BE PERSISTENT. YOU ARE GOING
TO HAVE ENCOUNTERS AND YOU ARE GOING
TO TAKE LUMPS - IT IS ALL A PART OF EARNING
YOUR *FIRE EATER* STRIPES. IF YOU ARE
KNOCKED DOWN, KEEP GETTING UP THAT
"ONE MORE TIME" BECAUSE YOU DO NOT
KNOW OR IDENTIFY WITH THE WORDS "TO BE
DEFEATED!"

9. ANALYSIS:

STAY AWAY FROM NEGATIVE INFLUENCES AT
ALL COSTS, YES, AT ALL COSTS! THEY ARE

DEVASTATING AND THEIR EFFECTS CAN
CAUSE INCALCULABLE DESTRUCTION. AND
REMEMBER, THERE ARE ONLY TWO CATEGO-
RIES OF PEOPLE: WINNERS AND NON-
WINNERS!

10. ANALYSIS:
DO NOT THINK YOU ARE A WINNER, BE
RECOGNIZED, ACKNOWLEDGED, A FULL-
FLEDGED, PROUD WINNER!

11. ANALYSIS:
BE READY WHEN OPPORTUNITY KNOCKS TO
OPEN THE DOOR WIDE. ALSO, LET YOUR
INTUITIVE FEELINGS HELP GUIDE YOU. WHEN
SOMETHING DOESN'T "FEEL" RIGHT, AVOID IT!

12. ANALYSIS:
SET A FIRE EATING GOAL THAT WILL MAKE
OTHERS SHUDDER AND TREMBLE JUST TO

THINK ABOUT IT. YOU CAN ACHIEVE IT BE-
CAUSE YOU ARE A *FIRE EATER*.

13. ANALYSIS:

I HAVE ALREADY SAID IT! GET IT! GET IT!

14. ANALYSIS:

DREAMS CAN BE CHANGED TO A REALITY AND
ONLY YOU HAVE THE *FIRE EATER* POWER TO
DO IT!

15. ANALYSIS:

A TRUE *FIRE EATER* IS NOT GREEDY. IN FACT,
YOU ENJOY SEEING OTHERS SUCCEED AS
LONG AS IT DOES NOT OBSCURE YOUR
SUCCESS.

16. ANALYSIS:

VISUALIZE: "SEE" YOUR DESTINY!

This list must be reviewed multiple times everyday. Not once a week, once a month, or once in a while - review it religiously on a daily basis. I cannot emphasize this point too much!

Go over these principles, go over these methods time and time again. Embed them in your mind. Visualize them in your mind. Think of them, then speak them aloud and let you hear yourself speaking them aloud. Then sit before a mirror and watch yourself speaking and listening to yourself studying these principles and programming them into your mind. Now you have total audio and visual input into yourself. Now you are becoming your own mechanism for biofeedback. You are now, in fact, programming your data banks in terms of the achievement of your success, in terms of your truly being transformed into the *FIRE EATER* that you were always meant to be. And let these principles be the last thing that you review before retiring to a sleep period and let them be first thing you review upon arising from your sleep. As you repetitiously review the chapter analyses, they will automatically become engraved in your subconscious. As you go through the audio phase of your own programming, they will become an integral part of your subconscious to the extent that you will no longer have to read them, that you will no longer have to recite them. Now they will be a part of your basic nature. You and the principles are one. You function as one and by knowing that you are the master of the principles you can now apply them at your own free will at your own discretion. Keep in mind that you get not what you want but what you subconsciously expect. You get what you project to others.

Again, I should emphasize that the brevity of this book is in no way a reflection of the impact it will have upon your life. Its brevity is, in fact, an asset! Merely because something is small does not mean that it is insignificant. Think of the trillions of cells in the human body containing trillions upon trillions of chemical compounds each being insignificant in and of itself yet their combination and confluence, is what leads to the actual life form known as the *FIRE EATER*. Thus, the principles herein may be brief but it is their combination which gives them their total overall stength - the creation of a *FIRE EATER*.

CHAPTER EIGHTEEN

Now That

You Have Arrived

"NOW THAT I HAVE ARRIVED"

I will press on. I will succeed. I am a *FIRE EATER*.
I will become that little drop in the bucket which accumulates until it becomes the raging surf.
I will be that ever so persistant little ant that devoured the carcass of the elephant.
I will be the weakling that was able to ring the sideshow bell because he needed to prove to himself that he could do it.
I will never accept defeat.
I will never consider defeat.
Defeat and/or failure will be eliminated from my vocabulary, just as non-winners ("losers") are not in my vocabulary.

I am made only to think the thoughts of the success of a *FIRE EATER*.

I will utilize every past perceived failure, every past hassle, every past liabiliy and turn them into a cumulative success, turn them into a cumulative asset, turn them into a cumulative accomplishment.

I will be the epitomy of an overachiever and I will be personally rewarded by my awareness of what I have achieved.

I know that with continued work and with continued effort that the flowers always blossom after a hard winter, that the grass is always greener where a barnyard once stood.

I am acutely aware that all success requires endurance and persistence and the ability to cope with what appears at times to be less than success, but with the makeup of a true *FIRE EATER*, it will be turned into undeniable success and achievement.

I will try as frequently as is necessary to overcome any and all obstacles in any conceiveable way with my being developed into a full-blown, fire eating, fire-breathing success.

I will utilize my time more efficiently and more effectively than any of my peers, than any of my competitors. In fact, my time utilization will be my "time warp." I will be so far ahead of the pack that I will not look toward them to judge my actions by their action. For then I would merely be slowed down to their pace. But, in fact, I will set my own fire eating, blistering, lighting fast, pace.

At the end of what others consider completion of a days work, I will press on at that time. I will utilize that time when they "tired" because I will not be tired because I will thrive on my success.

I will thrive on my achievements and I will thrive on the anticipation of even greater success.

Tiredness only exists in the mind for when the body is tired it will manifest the condition by collapse. It has built in pre-programmed fail-safe mechanisms to tell me when the body is tired.

74

I will not let the laziness of my body alter the assertiveness of my mind, alter the success-oriented direction of my nature. My mind will be in control of my body and my mind and my body, working in concert. It will be molding my destiny. Each day when I make that one last attempt to do more than the next individual has done or should have done, I realize that in doing so I am gaining an incredible advantage over those who stop at routine times, within routine bounds, with mundane goals. I will also realize, however, that with the attainment of any predetermined achievements, with any sought after success, that I will not just bask in the glory of that transitory success, but I will readily set my sights on the next target, on the next higher rung up the ladder because I am going to climb that ladder up to those unreachable stars even if I have to build the ladder as I go, build it rung by rung, build it step by step until I have held those beautiful stars in the palm of my hand.

I will press on. I will succeed. I am a *FIRE EATER*.

From my purely biochemical background, I realize that I am unique in many facets just as a canine can pick up my unique scent or trail, just as my finger print is unique, so is my approach to life itself, so is my approach to success, so is my full commitment to my life's work, to the molding of my destiny. I will utilize this uniqueness which I possess to augment my *FIRE EATER* approach.

I will utilize this uniqueness of self to convince others of my way of thinking.

I will utilize this uniqueness to increase my energy and effort expenditure daily, to increase the utilization of every possible neuron in my brain, to increase the output of every muscle fiber in my body.

I will press on. I will succeed. I am a *FIRE EATER*. I will push every muscle fiber to the point of exhaustion, beyond pain.

I will push every neuron to its maximal capacity, beyond strain. I will attempt to ascertain their limits of function. I will serve as my own greatest challenge. If and when those muscle fibers and if and when those neurons begin to ask for lenieney, I will demand of them greater energy and effort expenditure.

I will press on. I will succeed. I am a *FIRE EATER*.

With the achievement of each goal and with the attainment of each success, I will emerge even stronger than I was prior to the struggle. I will emerge victorious repeatedly, such that my next hurdle will be much more easily overcome. For now I have overcome inertia, momentum is my ally. The laws of Nature are working for me and I will utilize them to their fullest.

I will press on. I will succeed. I am a *FIRE EATER*.